DAREDEVILS

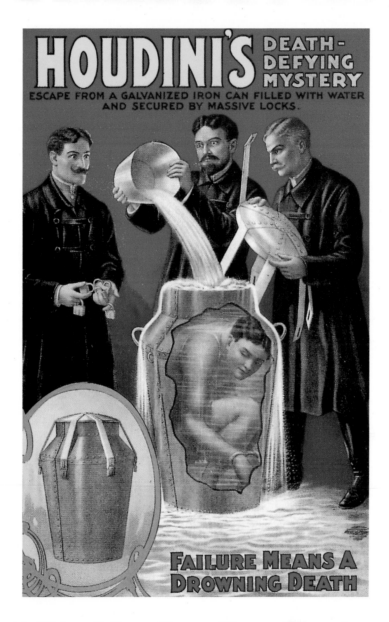

Edited by Caroline Clayton and Damian Kelleher

Written by Claire Watts

WORLD BOOK / TWO-CAN

DAREDEVILS

This edition published in
the United States in 1997
by World Book Inc.
525 W. Monroe
Chicago, IL 60661
in association with
Two-Can Publishing Ltd.

**For information on other World Book products,
call 1-800-255-1750, x 2238.**

ISBN: 0-7166-4502-5

Printed in Hong Kong

1 2 3 4 5 6 7 8 9 10 99 98 97 96

Design by Elizabeth Bell. Art directed by Catherine Page. Picture research by Debbie Dorman. Production by Lis Clegg.

Picture credits: Bob Thomas/Gamma/William Stevens 5; Bob Thomas 16; Mary Evans Picture Library 6; Topham 8; Mac Wilson/The Magic Circle 9c; Mander and Mitchenson Theatre Collection 9r; Robert Harding/Adina Tovy 10; Tony Stone/Chris Harvey 11; Kennywood Amusement Park 12bl; AAP/DPR Australia 12/13; Rex Features 13br, 14/15t, 25br, 26, 28; Jeffery R. Werner 14/15b; Zefa 17, 25tr; Kobal/EON Productions 18/19tc, 18bl; 19bl; Ronald Grant Archive/EON Productions 19br; Cliff Knox/Merrow Colour 20/21; Skyscraper Productions/John S. Harcourt 23t; Comstock Inc. 1992 23b; Stockfile/Steven Behr 27c; Camera Press/Mark Woolley 27r; Red Adair Co. 29; NASA/Britstock-Ifa 30tl; E. Bach/NASA/ Britstock-Ifa 30bl; Novosti 30bc; NASA/Science Photo Library 31.

Illustrations: Phil Gascoine, 4tr & bl, 5, 6/7, 17, 19, 22, 29; Joe Lawrence: 11, 15, 24; Chris Weston: 4tl. Lettering: John Aldritch.

CONTENTS

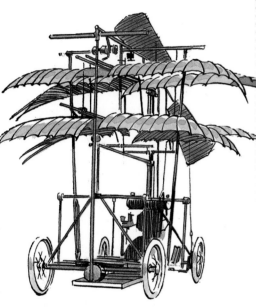

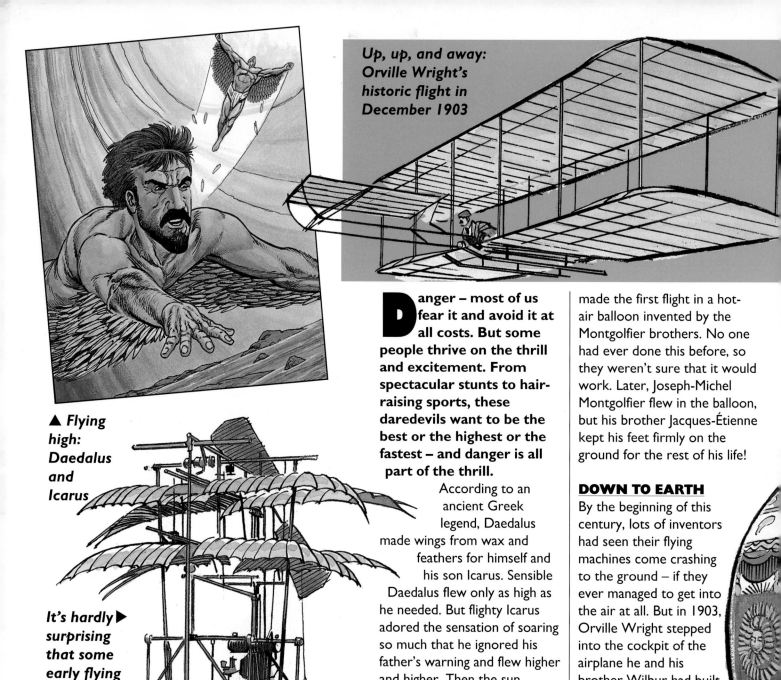

Up, up, and away: Orville Wright's historic flight in December 1903

▲ Flying high: Daedalus and Icarus

It's hardly▶ surprising that some early flying machines never got off the ground!

Danger – most of us fear it and avoid it at all costs. But some people thrive on the thrill and excitement. From spectacular stunts to hair-raising sports, these daredevils want to be the best or the highest or the fastest – and danger is all part of the thrill.

According to an ancient Greek legend, Daedalus made wings from wax and feathers for himself and his son Icarus. Sensible Daedalus flew only as high as he needed. But flighty Icarus adored the sensation of soaring so much that he ignored his father's warning and flew higher and higher. Then the sun melted his wings and he plunged headlong into the sea.

Perhaps Pilâtre de Rozier felt like Icarus when, in 1783, he made the first flight in a hot-air balloon invented by the Montgolfier brothers. No one had ever done this before, so they weren't sure that it would work. Later, Joseph-Michel Montgolfier flew in the balloon, but his brother Jacques-Étienne kept his feet firmly on the ground for the rest of his life!

DOWN TO EARTH

By the beginning of this century, lots of inventors had seen their flying machines come crashing to the ground – if they ever managed to get into the air at all. But in 1903, Orville Wright stepped into the cockpit of the airplane he and his brother Wilbur had built – still uncertain whether it would get off the ground – and made the first ever powered flight.

FEARLESS FIRSTS

Join in the thrills with the death-defying high-livers who dare to risk it all!

▲ Helmets on and heads down for some serious white-water rafting

ALL IN A DAY'S WORK

Being a daredevil is not just about being bold enough to take the plunge with a new invention. Some people risk their lives every day in their jobs. Steeplejacks climb high up the sides of chimneys and towers to repair them. Firefighters step into flaming buildings, braving infernos to save lives. You'd have to be a real daredevil to choose a job like that!

Show business can be an exciting way to make a living, too. From high-wire walkers to human cannonballs, it seems that some fame-seekers are prepared to do any kind of stunt to entertain an audience.

For others, being a daredevil is all about fun. Yes, sports like hang gliding, white-water rafting and ski jumping are thrilling to take part in – but they can be extremely dangerous, too. Do you have to be brave to be a daredevil, or just plain crazy? Read on and make up your own mind!

▲ We have liftoff: the amazing Montgolfier balloon

EL BOMBOS HUMAN CANNONBALL

◄ Human cannonballs take a shot at fame!

AMAZING MR. BLONDIN

The high-wire showman who walked – and pedaled and ate his way – across Niagara Falls!

Charles Blondin was determined to prove that he was the most daring tightrope walker the world had ever seen. No big-top tricks were good enough for him.

On June 30, 1859, Blondin had a rope 3 inches wide suspended 161 feet above the raging waters of Niagara Falls. That's about as high as 10 giraffes standing on top of one another! Then, in front of a huge crowd, he walked 1,100 feet across to the other side.

ONCE IS NOT ENOUGH!

Of course, everyone thought the French-born acrobat – real name Jean François Gravelet – was nutty to try such a dangerous stunt. But his circus training meant that he was no stranger to applause or risk, and Blondin loved nothing better than a crazy challenge! When others began to copy the daredevil feat, Blondin set about dreaming up wilder, even more hair-raising ways to cross the raging torrent.

He walked the tightrope on stilts. He pedaled over on a unicycle. He teetered across in a sack! Still he wasn't satisfied, and his amazing stunts became more outrageous. He pushed an assistant across in a wheelbarrow. He did it blindfolded. On one occasion, he even sat down and ate an omelette. No one could beat that!

OVER THE TOP

★ Niagara Falls has been the scene of many daredevil exploits. In 1901, Annie Edson Taylor "shot" the rapids of the Horseshoe Falls in a sealed, padded barrel and emerged unharmed. Since then, others have attempted the 177-foot drop, including Bob Leech (left). He went over the falls in a barrel in 1910 to win a bet!

THE GREAT

Harry Houdini, the man no chains could hold

Harry Houdini was the greatest escape artist the world has ever seen. He magically freed himself from ropes, chains, and handcuffs in death-defying stunts that dazzled audiences everywhere – and made his name a legend.

Houdini could escape from anything – even prison! In one display of his skills, he was locked inside a jail cell with his hands and feet chained together. To prove he had no hidden keys or equipment, he stripped to his underwear. Not only did Houdini escape, but when he reappeared he was fully clothed!

CHALLENGE HARRY

So confident was Houdini that he even challenged the public to come up with a device that would foil him. Many people tried and failed. One locksmith spent five years perfecting a pair of handcuffs he claimed "no mortal man could pick." It was one of Houdini's most difficult escapes – it took him a whole hour!

THE SECRETIVE STUNTMAN

But not all Houdini's stunts went according to plan. One of his most spectacular feats was escaping from a milk churn full of water with the lid padlocked on the outside. On one occasion he tried to escape from a churn filled with beer. While struggling to get out, he was overcome by the alcoholic fumes and fainted. The famous escape artist would have drowned if quick-thinking attendants hadn't smashed the locks and dragged him out.

Houdini was very careful not to reveal the secret of his tricks. Without a doubt, his assistants "fixed" some of the equipment, secretly undoing screws and weakening springs. But there was a lot more to Houdini's stunts than sneaky tricks.

He was an expert on locks and how to crack them. He was also incredibly strong and able to hold his breath underwater for several minutes. These were all part of the secret key to Houdini's astonishing stunts. But exactly how he performed some of them will always remain a mystery.

LIVING LEGEND DIES

Tragically, the man who narrowly escaped death a thousand times in his performances was killed by a terrible accident. A student named Gordon Whitehead punched Houdini to test the strength of his stomach muscles. But Houdini wasn't expecting the sudden blow and had no time to prepare himself.

The powerful punch burst Houdini's appendix. But even though the maestro was in terrible pain, he still managed to perform that same evening, though it was to be his last show. Two days later, on October 31, 1926, the world's greatest-ever escapologist died.

WEISS CHOICE!
Houdini's real name was Ehrich Weiss. He was born in Budapest, Hungary, in 1874, but he grew up in the United States. He changed his name in honor of his hero, the French magician Jean Eugene Robert-Houdin.

All tied up: Despite numerous padlocks and heavy, interlocking chains, Harry Houdini could always break loose.

ESCAPE

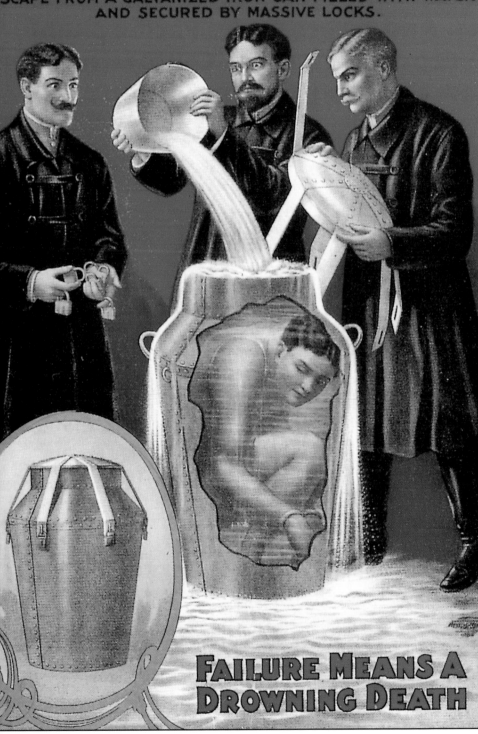

HOUDINI'S DEATH-DEFYING MYSTERY

ESCAPE FROM A GALVANIZED IRON CAN FILLED WITH WATER AND SECURED BY MASSIVE LOCKS.

FAILURE MEANS A DROWNING DEATH

WATER GREAT TRICK

The Chinese Water Torture Cell was perhaps Houdini's most famous and daring trick. His feet were locked into the lid of a huge, water-filled tank. He was then lowered headfirst into the water and the lid was sealed in place. Houdini had less than three minutes to free his feet and open the lid – from the inside – before he ran out of air. Very few modern magicians have dared to attempt this incredibly dangerous trick.

How did Houdini do it? Perhaps the answer lay in his amazing ability to hold his breath. But like all world-class performers, Houdini never let any of his secrets escape.

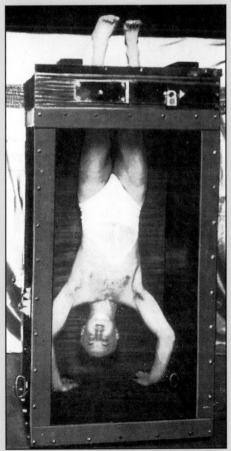

▲ Houdini's breathtaking Chinese Water Torture Cell trick

Waves sweep out from the high cliff. Just 21 feet out to sea, a jagged line of sharp rocks is clearly visible as each wave ebbs away.

The crowd gathered below is tense with excitement and fear. All eyes are fixed on a lone figure standing on a platform at the top of the cliff, waiting for his moment. Then, as the waves surge in over the rocks, he leaps off. The wide arc of his dive carries him 27 feet out to avoid the rocks. The crowd holds its breath until the diver's head breaks the surface and bobs up from the water. Then there is thunderous applause.

SAY A LITTLE PRAYER

Daredevil divers in Acapulco, Mexico, make this leap from the 87.5-foot-high La Quebrada cliffs every day in a spectacular display of bravery and good timing. La Quebrada, or "the break in the rocks," is a rocky cove only 12 feet deep, too shallow to dive into except when the waves come in. There are no steps in the cliff, so the divers have to climb up the steep rock face.

A new diver usually starts at the age of fourteen. An experienced La Quebrada diver teaches him to judge the timing of the waves and to land in the right way to protect his face and stomach from the impact of the water. Often, it's an older brother or a cousin who acts as his teacher – diving at La Quebrada is a family business! At first, the new recruit dives from lower down the rocks. Then, gradually, he dives from higher and higher up the cliffs until he is ready to take his first leap from the very top.

A BREATH-TAKING LEAP

Mexican high-fliers risk death on the rocks. And divers in the Pacific plumb the depths for pearls. Can't fathom how they do it? Then read on . . .

▲ *Hold your nose! The death-defying dive of the La Quebrada daredevils*

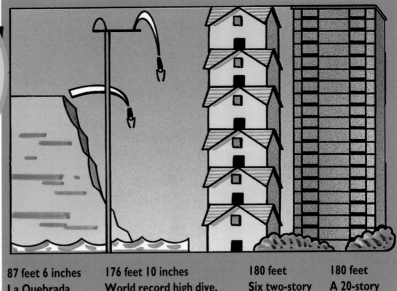

| 87 feet 6 inches La Quebrada cliffs | 176 feet 10 inches World record high dive, Olivier Favre, Aug 30, 1987 | 180 feet Six two-story houses | 180 feet A 20-story building |

Most of us can hold our breath underwater for only a few seconds. The official world record is two minutes, 46 seconds. But in the tropical seas of the Pacific, people regularly dive to depths of over 100 feet with no breathing aids at all, searching for valuable pearls and sponges.

In Japan and Korea, the women who free-dive for pearls are known as *amas*. The divers plunge down, grab whatever pearl shells or sponges come within their reach and come up as quickly as they can, gasping for air.

The pearl divers of Polynesia have made their job slightly easier. They wear goggles made from pieces of transparent turtle shell, set in disks of hollow bamboo, so that they can see what they are doing underwater.

BEWARE OF THE BENDS

The pressure of water above someone diving to such great depths can be very dangerous. When the diver comes up to the surface, nitrogen in his or her bloodstream causes bubbles, which interrupt the blood flow. This can cause terrible muscular spasms, breathing problems, or even paralysis – conditions divers call "the bends."

▲ *Hold your breath! On the hunt for treasure down among the coral*

..AND A BREATH-HOLDING DIVE!

WHITE KN

It's a wild whirl! The corkscrew at Seaworld in Queensland, Australia

The car climbs up the steep track. Beneath it, the flimsy-looking wood and metal structure rattles and creaks. At the top, the car pauses and the "joyriders" look at the ant-sized people standing in line below. Suddenly, the car lurches forward and plunges down at a speed of up to 80 miles per hour. The passengers are pressed back into their seats, gasping for breath and clutching on for dear life. No wonder they call it a white-knuckle ride!

Roller coasters can be unbelievably scary, but that's all part of the fun. They are built to rigorous safety standards and checked regularly for any faults. The wheels of the cars are designed to clamp onto the steel tracks, so that even if they stopped upside down, the cars would not fall off.

MURDER IN THE DARK!
Taller, faster, and scarier roller coasters are being built all the time. Some, like the Space Mountain ride at Walt Disney World whizz through completely dark buildings with just a few flashing lights and illuminated stars. Passengers have no idea which direction they are traveling in, just a fantastic sensation of speed.

But if tummy turmoil is your idea of fun, the Steel Phantom at Kennywood Amusement Park in Pittsburgh, Pennsylvania, is the ultimate thrill. It has the world's greatest roller coaster drop – 225 feet. That's the same as swooping down from a 25-story building!

Yikes – the Steel Phantom's 225-foot drop is the world's longest – and scariest!

UCKLES

★ Ever wondered why you don't fall out of a roller coaster?

When you're whizzing around upside down, you can feel a force pushing you toward your seat. When an object is set in motion, it will continue moving in a straight line unless something causes it to change direction. By traveling in a circle, your direction is constantly being changed. The force you feel keeping you in your seat is trying to make you move in a straight line.

This is called centripetal force. You could fall out of the roller coaster only if it stopped or began to move too slowly. Luckily, you would be strapped to your seat to stop that from happening!

▲ How about a ride upside down at 80 miles per hour?

Eddie Kidd and Robbie Knievel are world-famous for their daredevil motorcycle stunts. It's no wonder they're called . . .

THE JUMPING

Bay St. Louis, Mississippi, July 9, 1993. Two of the world's most famous motorcycle daredevils came face-to-face in a modern-day clash of the Titans. Their challenge: to jump the farther distance in a total of three leaps. The victor: Eddie Kidd – by a whisker! His three jumps totaled 631 feet. Robbie Knievel's three attempts added up to a total distance of 625 feet. That makes Eddie Kidd the new world champion of motorcycle jumping.

It was close. Like Eddie, Robbie Knievel was born to ride dangerously. Two decades ago, his father, Evel Knievel, leaped to fame over rows of cars and buses on his Harley Davidson bike. Knievel Senior cleared 52 wrecked cars, zoomed over 13 side-by-side double-decker buses, and even leaped across a tank full of hungry sharks. In performing these stunts he claims to have broken more than 100 bones.

BOY WONDER
Britain's Eddie Kidd admits that it was Evel Knievel who inspired him to become a stunt rider. As a boy he saw Evel's film, *Viva Knievel*, and began to practice daring leaps on his bicycle. He soon proved himself a match for first his hero and later his hero's son. Since the day he successfully cleared 14 double-decker buses, Eddie has soared over treacherous ravines, railroad bridges, and even the Great Wall of China.

Now Robbie's arrival on the daredevil scene has kept the rivalry alive. The 1993 challenge in Bay St. Louis put Eddie one jump ahead of Robbie. But how long will it be before his revving rival catches up?

Robbie Knievel – motorcycle daredevil ▶

▲ *The Kidd caught in midflight*

▶ *Who left those boxes there? Eddie breaks his fall on a cardboard crash barrier.*

GIANTS

JUMP TO IT

★ On June 22, 1991, American Doug Danger zoomed in to *The Guinness Book of Records*. He jumped his motorcycle over 251 feet and rode away with the ramp-jumping record.

251 feet is ▶ equal to just over 30 cars or eight buses or longer than a couple of whopping blue whales. That's some leap!

HOLD ON!

Rock climbing is a pretty hair-raising sport when you have ropes to keep you from falling too far. But imagine doing it with no safety equipment!

Free-climbing, or soloing as it is also called, is a sport that takes a lot of nerve. But these fearless climbers seem to hang on to the rock as easily as a fly crawls up the wall. Free from ropes, they climb with bare hands and no protective headgear. So what's the secret of their amazing skill?

To be a champion climber takes fingers of steel, and many climbers spend hours exercising their hands. Some even practice pulling their whole bodies up with just one finger!

Most climbers train on indoor climbing walls or even on holds they have set in garage walls and ceilings at home. And specially molded training walls, up to 100 feet high, can be as hard to climb as the real thing.

MISSION IMPOSSIBLE

One of the most demanding places for free-climbing is Yosemite Valley, California. To an untrained eye the sheer, smooth rock faces look impossible to climb, but the determined can always find a route up! Climbing without ropes is kinder to the landscape because bolts don't need to be attached to the rock.

◀ *Dangling with danger: the thrill of free-climbing*

GRIPPING INSIDE INFO

★ How do climbers ascend a smooth rock face? They start by making their way up the rock using cracks and holding on to knobs of stone. They place their feet sideways on any tiny piece of rock that sticks out to give them a firmer hold.

Most climbers say it's where their hands go that matters most – feet tend to find their own grips. Once their feet have a firm hold, they stretch a hand upward to find a new, higher grip.

THE HEIGHT OF FASHION

One hundred years ago, a British woman climber named Lucy Walker scaled nearly 100 high mountains, including the Matterhorn and Mont Blanc. In spite of her daring, she did conform to some of the ideas of the time: she wore a long dress to climb in and took champagne and sponge cake to eat on the summit!

Modern mountaineers choose much more practical gear these days. For scaling summits in snow and ice, they wear warm, waterproof clothing and take along ice picks, spikes, boots, and ropes. Although they don't take champagne and cake, they do carry supplies of high-energy food just in case they get stuck.

STUNNING S

It's the spectacular stunts in James Bond films and other action-packed movies that keep the audience gasping

In the opening scene of the James Bond movie *For Your Eyes Only*, fearless super-spy 007 is seen perilously clinging to a swaying helicopter. In *Moonraker*, our hero looks as cool as a cucumber as he hangs by a thread from a soaring cable car.

But Bond fans are watching an illusion. It's not actor Roger Moore risking life and limb for the sake of a stunning stunt. Behind each gripping moment is a stunt double. These are specially trained actors who are brought in to do dangerous scenes in movies and television shows.

> **66 Being a stunt performer isn't just about being a daredevil 99**

Although many leading actors enjoy doing their own stunts, it's not always a good idea. One false move and the stunt could result in injury. For this reason, producers turn to stunt doubles of the same height or build as the actors — convincing look-alikes who can act out hazardous scenes.

DOUBLE O DOUBLE!

Stuntman Martin Grace has doubled for Roger Moore in five Bond movies and stepped in to take numerous punches for all-action actors like Harrison Ford. "I've also been set on fire from head to toe and been thrown out of skyscraper windows!"

But even though the stunts look very dangerous, safety is the key to a successful career. "Being a stunt performer isn't just about being a daredevil," Martin explains. "It takes a great deal of training. You must have at least six stunt qualifications, which include things like free-fall parachuting, martial arts, scuba diving, and horse riding."

Stunt people also need plenty of acting experience. So before you become the next James Bond Junior, take Martin Grace's advice: "A head for hard work is just as important as a head for heights in this job!"

Trick photography and slow motion are the keys to realistic star shots. Here Roger Moore is filmed clinging to a moving train in Octopussy.

Stunt double Martin Grace throws himself into action in The Spy Who Loved Me *(above).*

18

STUNTS

Many action-packed films, such as *Raiders of the Lost Ark*, are famous for incredibly realistic stunts. But it takes more than just a convincing double to pull off a stunt. The way a scene is shot can make the difference between a box-office smash or a film flop!

The stunt is filmed in two positions in order to get close-ups of the actor, plus high silhouette shots.

▶ **1** First, the actor is safely harnessed to the edge and filmed clinging on from above. This shows the height of the fall and makes the audience believe the actor is doing the stunt.

◀ **2** A safe landing pad is then set up where the stunt performer will fall, using layers of empty cardboard boxes or a huge, inflatable mattress.

◀ **3** The stunt double takes the actor's position and is filmed from the ground up.

▶ **4** As he falls, he cleverly turns his body away from the camera so that he isn't recognized.

◀ **5** The landing pad is removed, the real actor is placed in position, and he is filmed from high up again to show the drop of the fall.

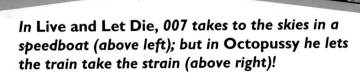

In **Live and Let Die**, *007 takes to the skies in a speedboat (above left); but in* **Octopussy** *he lets the train take the strain (above right)!*

B eing a pilot is a very skilled job – but imagine having to fly upside down with eight other planes coming right at you! Some pilots perform aerobatics just for the thrill of it. But these loopy loopers are part of a crack team who show off their breathtaking skills at airshows.

BOMB BURST

Controlled by a leader, stunt planes can fly in many different formations. Our picture shows a formation called the Bomb Burst, performed here by Great Britain's Royal Air Force aerobatic team, the Red Arrows. The planes trail colored smoke so that watchers on the ground can see them more easily.

Aircraft used for aerobatic displays need extrastrong wings so that they work as well upside down as they do right side up. They need to be fast,

too – the Red Arrows' Hawk jets can fly at up to 650 miles per hour.

Aerobatic teams only perform in good weather, because the slightest wind can buffet one plane into another. If a plane is badly positioned, or if something goes wrong, the pilots can talk to one another on two-way radios fitted inside their helmets.

Aerobatic pilots train in planes with dual controls. The instructor sits behind the trainee pilot so that if any stunts begin to go wrong, he can take over. Roger and out!

WINGED W

It's those magnificent men in their flying

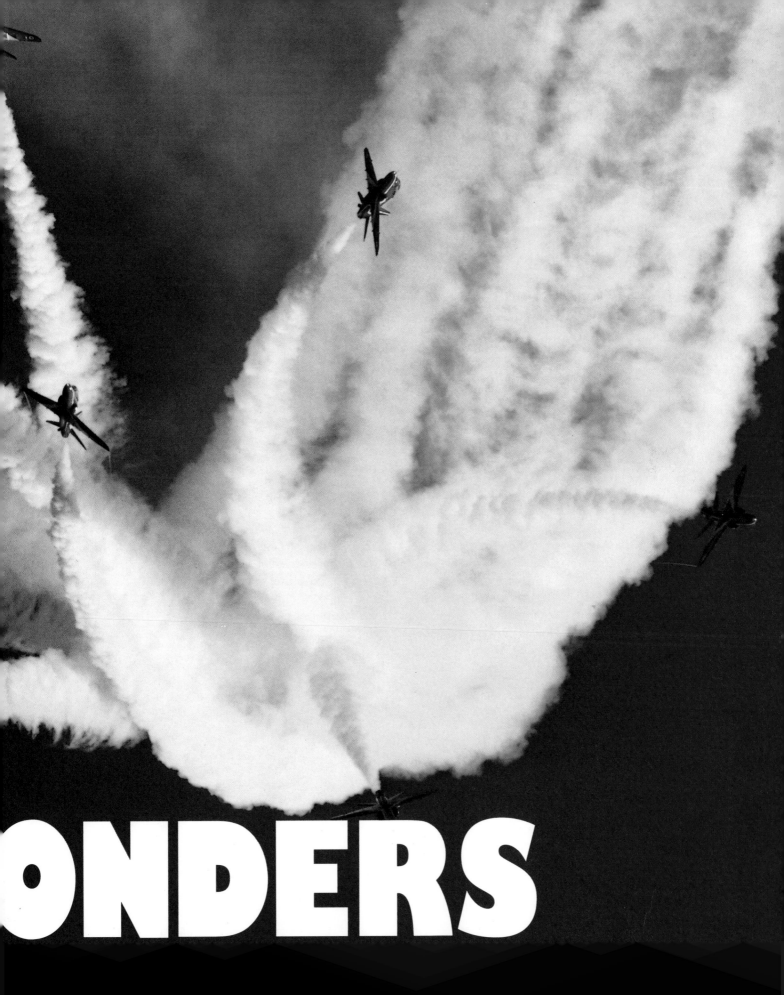

ONDERS

JUST PLANE CRAZY

Not long after airplanes were invented, people began to perform aerobatic stunts. At first, it was thought that if a plane flew upside down, the wings would fall off!

But on August 27, 1913, Lt. Capt. Nikolayevich Nesterov of the Imperial Russian Air Service disproved all that. He managed to loop the loop in a Nieuport Type IV monoplane. A month later, Frenchman Célestin-Adolphe Pégoud made the point again when he flew his Blériot airplane upside down. Because planes didn't have seatbelts in those days, pilots tied themselves in with ropes so that they wouldn't fall out when they were upside down!

WALKING IN THE AIR
Soon, flying circuses became fashionable. To the roar of the crowd, pilots would loop the loop and fly upside down. They flew under low bridges

Wing-walkers fly high with just their feet strapped in. Yikes!

and faked crashes, pulling up at the last moment. Acrobats performed while hanging from the undercarriages of the planes or standing on top of the wings.

Planes even flew close together so that their wings almost touched and people could walk across from one plane to another!

Things did not always go as planned, though, and there was the ever-present danger of the flimsy planes tumbling to the ground and exploding in a fast-burning fire of wood and fabric.

WATCH OUT! Nowadays, stunt flyers are not allowed to fly too near the ground – they could put the lives of spectators in jeopardy.

IS IT A BIRD? NO, IT'S A PLANE!
Here's how some of those ace aerobatics are achieved

◀ Falling leaf
Plane plummets down headfirst, then pulls up at the last moment.

Roll ▲
The plane twists itself around in a corkscrew movement as it flies along in the sky.

Loop ▶
Plane flies up, over on its back, down and back around to its original path.

Hundreds of feet above the busy streets of New York City, Mohawk Indians move around on the huge metal skyscraper skeletons they are building.

These skilled metalworkers spend all day on the buildings, up to 800 feet off the ground. They stride along beams just 6 inches wide without a safety harness to keep them from plummeting to the ground if they make a wrong move.

DAREDEVIL SKILLS

How did the Mohawks learn this amazing skill? For hundreds of years, Native Americans have crossed deep streams and treacherous ravines on the narrowest logs. There was no other way for the Mohawks to cross these hazards, so they learned to develop a head for heights that now comes as second nature.

WALKING TALL

The Mohawks' daredevil skill was first used commercially in 1886, when they were hired to help build a high railroad bridge near their reservation. They walked around on it so calmly that they were soon being trained for skilled metalworking jobs. Today, there are Mohawks at work on many soaring structures being built in New York City.

FEARLESS!
The American Indian tribe with an astonishing head for heights

Cool and casual, Mohawk construction workers don't flinch an inch while working on the world's tallest buildings.

23

THE SKY'S THE LIMIT!

Got a head for heights? Then meet the surfers with their heads in the clouds!

WHAT A DROP!

See how far the sky surfers fall

Jump from aircraft 12,000 feet

The parachute opens here 2,000 feet

Sears Tower (the world's second tallest building) 1,454 feet

Imagine looking out of an airplane window and seeing someone sail past – on a surfboard! Well if it happens, don't worry. It's probably just a sky surfer riding the tide 12,000 feet up in the air!

THE THRILL OF IT ALL

Sky surfing is a current craze that's strictly for the professionals. A sky surfer jumps out of a plane and cruises along in its slipstream on a surfboard at speeds of up to 100 miles per hour. Riding the thermal currents in the atmosphere, you can surf on the air, just like on water!

SHORT SHARP SURF

But be warned – if it's a longer-lasting thrill you're seeking, then this isn't the sport for you. Just 40 seconds after diving out, with a pull on the ripcord, the surfer drifts safely down to Earth on his parachute. Many enthusiasts of this new sport started off skydiving but have given it all up for surfing. In fact, you could say they just got "board"!

▲ Open the hatch – surf's up!

HEAD FIRST!

Sky surfing is a type of skydiving – a sport for the most daring of daredevils! Falling headfirst out of the sky, divers can reach speeds of up to 185 miles per hour!

After about a minute of free-falling, the sky diver opens his parachute. This acts as an air brake and slows the fall down to about 11 miles per hour.

ALL JOIN HANDS

★ Moving around in the air during a free-fall, or "tracking," is quite simple. You just use your arms and legs like rudders to move across the sky. In July 1992, 150 sky divers tracked across the sky to join hands and feet in the largest ever free-fall formation (below).

STACKING THEM UP

Getting close together when your parachute is already open is much more dangerous. Modern ram-air parachutes have steering cords to move them right, left, up, or down. If parachute strings get twisted together, all 323 square feet of the parachute can collapse. But that didn't stop these 24 members of the Royal Marine Free-Fall Display Team from joining up in the world's highest parachute stack (right).

▲ Who says you need sea to surf? Dry high-fliers are taking to the skies for the ultimate experience.

▲ READY... Stand on the edge of the platform. An elastic rope, or bungee cord, is attached to a full-body harness.

▲ SET... Step forward off the platform and plunge down...

GOING... GOING... GONE!

It takes a strong piece of elastic and a lot of nerve to go bungee jumping!

In 1979, David Kirk of the **Dangerous Sports Club** started a wild new craze when he jumped off the Clifton Suspension Bridge, near Bristol, England.

Attached to his ankle was nothing more than an elastic rope. No wonder everyone thought he was nuts!

Now, a few years later, it seems everybody's doing it. Bungee jumping is bouncy, stomach-churning fun. From a bridge or a crane, in a wheelchair or on a bike, it's a sport that has all sorts of people diving off tall platforms and daring to dangle upside down by the ankles.

GO! Down she drops, ▶ dunking her head in the water. Then, as the elastic rope jerks back up, she soars away again in the opposite direction!

THE FIRST BUNGEE JUMPERS?

★ Every year, the men of Pentecost Island in the Pacific perform a death-defying ritual that's remarkably similar to bungee jumping.

Standing 100 feet up on a rickety, wooden tower, the jumpers throw themselves off, headfirst, as part of an ancient ceremony. Just as they are about to hit the ground, they bounce back up, leaping onto a hillside to safety. How on earth do they do it?

Before they jump, the men's ankles are tied to the top of the tower with a stretchy kind of creeper called a *liana*. This strong attachment is the only thing that saves the Pentecost Island divers from a certain death. Maybe David Kirk's idea wasn't so original after all!

Taking the plunge on Pentecost Island

Bungee jumping isn't for beginners. Don't even think about trying this kind of stunt at home!

RED ALERT!

He's the world's most famous firefighter with the most dangerous job on the planet. But beating the heat is all in a day's work for Red Adair.

Faced with more than 700 oil fires after the Gulf War, the Kuwaiti government got on the hotline to the world's favorite flame buster, Red Adair. Red tackled his first oil-well fire at the age of twenty-five. Since then, he has made his name fighting the most dangerous oil and gas fires around the globe.

SLOW BURN

In 1961, Red was called to Algeria. Out in the desert, an oil-well fire nicknamed The Devil's Cigarette Lighter had been burning for almost six months and could be seen 100 miles away. Geologists said there was enough oil below it to burn for 100 years. Gas shot out of the well 450 feet into the air faster than the speed of sound. The flame was so hot it was turning the desert sand to glass.

Red and his team used a bulldozer to drop a barrel of explosives into the mouth of the well, then ran for cover. There was a massive explosion, then the smoke cleared and the fire was out. While a constant stream of water poured down on them, the gang worked day and night until the well was finally capped.

PIPER ALPHA

On July 6, 1988, the Piper Alpha oil rig in the North Sea burst into a sheet of flames. It burned so bright that the inferno was visible over 80 miles away. It was the worst offshore oil platform disaster ever.

The platform was burning at over 1,800°F, so the problem was, how could anyone get close enough to put the fires out? Red Adair was the man for the job! Adair used water cannons to provide a protective blanket of water for his emergency ship. Then he pumped seawater onto the platform to douse the furious flames.

Once the fires were out, seawater was pumped down the oil pipes. When oil stopped flowing out, cement was pumped down to seal the well. Red and his team had put out the Piper Alpha inferno in just 36 days.

DESERT QUENCH

Red's toughest challenge came at the end of the Gulf War in 1991. As the Iraqi army retreated, it set fire to more than 700 Kuwaiti oil wells. All over the country, flames shot hundreds of feet into the air, covering much of Kuwait with a cloud of dense smoke. Twelve thousand men, most of the world's professional oil firefighters, were called in to take part in Operation Desert Quench.

Red predicted that it would take five years to put out all the fires. All sorts of odd methods were suggested, from towing in an iceberg to shooting rockets down the wells. In fact, the operation took only eight months, using the tried and tested method of pumping seawater and mud into the wells.

◀ Adair-devil in action: Red supervises the capping of a Kuwaiti oil well.

HOW RED ADAIR PUTS OUT AN OIL-WELL FIRE

▲ In dozens of years of fire fighting, Red Adair has put out thousands of fires. But what does the hero have to say for himself? "I'm not a daredevil," he told an interviewer, "I'm a beware-devil."

**ANY COLOR...
AS LONG AS IT'S RED**
Red's real name is Paul, but he's called Red because his hair was once the color of carrots and he always wears red clothes to work!

SPACE ADVEN

The brave pioneers who blazed a trail into the unknown – outer space!

▲ *What goes up...* Apollo 15/Saturn V *blasts off in 1971 and* Apollo 16 *splashes down in the Pacific Ocean in 1972.*

He was going to a place where no one had ever been before... and no one could be sure that he would ever return.

On April 12, 1961, Yuri Gagarin of the Soviet Union became the first person to go into space. *Vostok I*, his spacecraft, reached a height of 203 miles. His flight lasted just 108 minutes before he landed safely in Russia.

Before Gagarin's flight, no one was sure whether the human body would be able to stand the rigors of space travel. First, the body feels as though it's being crushed by the force of the launching rocket. Then, immediately afterward, it has to cope with weightlessness.

Since Gagarin, there have

▲ *Yuri Gagarin, the first person to go up into space*

been more than 150 manned flights into space: Astronauts have walked on the moon, lived in special space stations for over a year, and even docked two space craft together in orbit, 137 miles up.

Space voyages have allowed astronauts to travel faster than ever before, at speeds of up to 25,000 miles per hour. That's faster than a speeding bullet! But with some 700 tons of flammable fuel in their tanks on liftoff, the smallest problem could turn into a major disaster.

On January 28, 1986, a U.S. space launch ended in tragedy. The fuel tank of the space shuttle *Challenger* exploded 73 seconds after liftoff at a height of 47,000 feet. The entire crew of seven, including schoolteacher Christa McAuliffe, was killed.

STRETCH IN SPACE

The first astronauts were intrepid explorers facing unknown dangers. But today, advanced technology and expertise have made space travel much safer. To cope with all kinds of testing situations that may arise, astronauts need to be at the peak of physical fitness. That's why their training program covers everything from control of the spacecraft to coping with weightlessness, plus some exhausting workouts thrown in for good measure!

IT'S A GAS!

On February 7, 1984, U.S. astronaut Bruce McCandless floated free in space, the first person to spacewalk without attachment to his craft. He relied totally on his gas-propelled Manned Maneuvering Unit to get him safely back to Challenger.

INDEX